The Unconscious

Phil Mollon

Series editor: Ivan Ward

ICON BOOKS UK
TOTEM BOOKS USA

Published in the UK in 2000 by Icon Books Ltd., Grange Road, Duxford, Cambridge CB2 4QF email: info@iconbooks.co.uk www.iconbooks.co.uk

Published in the USA in 2001 by Totem Books Inquiries to: Icon Books Ltd., Grange Road, Duxford, Cambridge CB2 4QF, UK

Distributed in the UK, Europe, Canada, South Africa and Asia by the Penguin Group: Penguin Books Ltd., 27 Wrights Lane, London W8 5TZ

In the United States, distributed to the trade by National Book Network Inc., 4720 Boston Way, Lanham, Maryland 20706

Published in Australia in 2000 by Allen & Unwin Pty. Ltd., PO Box 8500, 9 Atchison Street, St. Leonards, NSW 2065

Library of Congress catalog card number applied for

Text copyright © 2000 Phil Mollon

The author has asserted his moral rights.

Series editor: Ivan Ward

ISBN 1 84046 187 X

Typesetting by Hands Fotoset

Printed and bound in the UK by Cox & Wyman Ltd., Reading

The concept of the unconscious has long been knocking at the gates of psychology and asking to be let in. Philosophy and literature have often toyed with it, but science could find no use for it. (Freud, 1940)[1]

The lewd interloper

A man approaches the ticket desk of an airline in the USA intending to buy tickets to Pittsburgh and is served by an extremely attractive young woman endowed with very ample breasts. Somewhat flustered, the man blurts out 'Two pickets to Tittsburgh please!' His mistake reveals, in a rather obvious fashion, desires other than his *conscious* wish to purchase a ticket for his journeys.[2] A competing lust has lewdly interlocuted, disrupting his speech.

An author, highly irritated by some of his editor's suggestions for changes to the submitted text, dutifully complied with the request and revised the manuscript. He then attempted to send the new version to the editor by e-mail. Some days later, not having heard from the editor, he phoned to enquire and discovered that the e-mail had not been received. He then checked his e-mail folder and found, to his acute embarrassment, that he had mailed it to another publisher's address! Although this had not been his conscious intention, his mistaken action was congruent with a wishful fantasy of turning to an alternative publisher. A competing intention had infiltrated and hijacked the writer's actions.

Towards the end of the nineteenth century, the President of the Austrian Parliament opened a sitting with the words: 'I take notice that a full quorum of members is present and herewith declare the sitting *closed*.'[3] Naturally, what he intended consciously to say was that the sitting was open, but instead he made a slip of the tongue which revealed what he really felt. A number of the sittings of the House shortly before had been stormy and unproductive, so it would be understandable that the President would far rather he were making his closing rather than opening speech. Although intending to *open* the sitting, a competing wish expressed itself instead.

In such ways the unconscious speaks – often embarrassingly, as if in humiliating mockery of our illusions of conscious awareness and control over our desires and intentions. Consciousness can appear as merely a fragile bubble on the deep waters of emotion, desire and fear.

Is the unconscious a valid concept?

The unconscious is by definition unknowable ... The

psychoanalyst is therefore in the unfortunate position of being a student of that which cannot be known.[4]

The idea of unconscious motivation is an inference that provides an explanation for the gaps and distortions in our consciousness. This hypothesis, which brings coherence to behavioural and mental data that would otherwise appear incoherent, was first explored systematically by Sigmund Freud. He saw that slips of the tongue or pen, failures of memory, bungled actions and other mistakes can be, at a deeper level, not random errors but unconsciously intended. His genius was to see that such seemingly trivial phenomena were worth studying, and moreover to recognise the link between these and other mental creations like dreams, jokes and neurotic symptoms.

People sometimes express scepticism about the existence of an unconscious mind – as if reasoning along the lines of 'If we cannot perceive something with our consciousness then it does not exist'. Certainly, 'the unconscious' can seem an elusive concept. By definition, if a part of the mind is unconscious then we are not conscious of it. Does that mean that a hypothesis, or 'interpretation', regarding an unconscious content of the mind is completely beyond scrutiny in the light of evidence – a pronouncement inspired by dogma and to be swallowed by the patient unquestioningly on the supposed 'authority' of the psychoanalyst? Fortunately, the epistemological position is not quite so bleak. It is possible to think in terms of *gradations* of consciousness. In the examples given above, the individual's competing intentions were not very far from consciousness.

A moment's introspection, combined with a minimal degree of psychological mindedness, would have brought the less conscious wish into the person's full awareness. Similarly, in the course of psychoanalytic therapy, where the patient is encouraged to speak and think freely as far as possible, his or her previously unconscious wishes and fears become gradually closer to consciousness.

A psychoanalytic interpretation that went quite beyond the patient's potential awareness, so that it could only be accepted on faith, would be quite useless. Interpretations given in analysis are tentative hypotheses about what might be going on in the patient's mind, or between patient and analyst. They are based on the evidence of the patient's behaviour and words, and are assessed in the light of the patient's response.

Psychoanalysis is a cooperative venture undertaken by analyst and patient with the aim of expanding the domain of consciousness, so that the latter can conduct his or her life with more awareness, freedom and choice. However, it is a journey of exploration into the unknown, in which any sense of certainty must be eschewed.

The question of the plausibility of the unconscious can be turned around. We might ask instead, 'How plausible is it that we are conscious of all our mental processes?' or 'What is the function of *consciousness*?' For most of its history, experimentally based psychology has been as uncomfortable with the notion of consciousness as it has of unconsciousness, since both have seemed beyond the scope of laboratory investigation.

Radical behaviourists of the early twentieth century regarded consciousness as merely an 'epiphenomenon', without scientific significance or interest.[5] As more sophisticated psychology has developed, both consciousness and unconsciousness have become open to scientific investigation of their processes and functions.[6]

The idea of consciousness is actually similar to that of attention. We are conscious of what we attend to, and not conscious of what we do not attend to. We could become conscious of some things quite easily if we turned our attention to them – corresponding to what Freud[7] called the 'preconscious'. We might actively avoid attending to other things because we find them painful or disturbing – the repressed unconscious.

Perhaps a contemporary analogy might help. Consciousness could be compared to what is visible on a computer screen. Other information could be accessed readily by scrolling down the document or by switching to a different 'window'. This would be analogous to the conscious and the preconscious parts of the mind. However, some files on the computer may be less easily explored. They may have been encrypted or 'zipped', or they may require a password or are in other ways rendered 'access denied'. Some may also have been corrupted, so that information is scrambled and thereby rendered incomprehensible. While the Internet potentially makes available (to people collectively) all kinds of information and images (analogous to Jung's 'collective unconscious'), a programme may have been installed that restricts access to Internet sites, *censoring* some that contain material considered unacceptable. Moreover, most of the activity of the computer is not visible on the screen; this is analogous to Freud's idea of the bodily based instincts, or 'id',[8] in themselves inaccessible to the mind, only to be discerned through their derivatives (desires and phantasies).

Yet another aspect of the unconscious is suggested by the peculiar frustration that this writer personally experienced in the early stages of getting to grips with a computer and in my initial attempts to access the Internet. I felt at times utterly bewildered. What added to the agony of this perplexity was that I could not even begin to identify and formulate in words the questions for which I needed the answers; at times it seemed that nothing made sense. This is analogous to what might be termed the 'presymbolic unconscious'[9] – those areas of experience of which we cannot be properly conscious because we have not been able to generate words or any other form of mental representation of them. These phenomena may at times be associated with anxiety, perplexity or 'presymbolic dread'. The concept of the presymbolic unconscious would also apply to earliest infancy before the development of language.

Farts, stains and lies

Other examples of slips of the tongue bring us closer to the realm of psychological illness or psychopathology.

A patient was referred to a clinic with an exaggerated fear of losing control of his bowels and an associated persisting pain in his anus (although there appeared to be no physical abnormality). The psychotherapist asked the man to describe more about this problem and how it was experienced. In speaking of his fear of losing control and expelling faeces or flatus, the man inadvertently said he was afraid of letting his 'feelings' out. This was almost certainly not what he consciously intended to say, but it did accurately express his unconscious anxieties. It provided a clue, which then enabled the psycho-therapist to enquire about certain areas of the patient's life that could be troubling him emotionally.

The patient acknowledged that he did at times experience worry about a particular problem, but he said he tried to expel such thoughts from his mind. Thus, his worries were evacuated into his body, but the problem was merely displaced. A common example of a similar process is that of a child complaining of physical discomfort, such as a tummy ache, when worried about school or some other situation.

Another patient experienced states of panic at work when in the presence of his boss. In describing these he stumbled over his words, saying: 'I had a ang . . .

anxiety attack.' Further exploration revealed that he was indeed troubled by conflicts over his feelings of *anger* towards his boss (which were derived from earlier feelings of anger towards his father) – and that it was his unconscious fear of his anger bursting out that led to his anxiety.

A second window into the unconscious is revealed by an unravelling of the meaning of seemingly bizarre and inexplicable neurotic symptoms. Freud[10] gives the following example of a severe obsessional neurosis.

A lady of thirty years of age felt compelled to repeat a particular action many times each day: she would run from one room to another one, take up a particular position beside a table, ring the bell for her housemaid, send her on some errand, then run back into her own room. Initially, neither Freud nor the patient had the faintest idea what on earth this ritual was about. However, the lady eventually provided the crucial clue. Ten years previously she had married a man who was impotent on their wedding night. On several occasions throughout the night he had to run from his room to hers in order to try again to have intercourse, but without success.

In the morning he had declared angrily that he would feel ashamed in front of the housemaid when she made the bed if there were no evidence of sexual activity. He had then procured a bottle of red ink and poured some of it over the sheet, although not quite in the right place where a blood stain would have been appropriate. Having told Freud this account, the lady then took him into the room where she would sit at her table during her ritual. She showed him a big red stain on the tablecloth. Apparently she would sit at the table in such a position that the stain was immediately apparent to the maid whom she summoned.

Freud's explanation of the obsessional ritual, in the light of this information, was as follows. The patient was identifying with her husband in her act of running from room to room. The table and tablecloth represented the bed and sheet. Thus the patient's ritual appeared to be a representation and repetition of the wedding night scenes. Through summoning the maid before whose eyes the stain was displayed, she was symbolically both repeating the scene and putting it right – the stain was in the right place. According to Freud's interpretation, the obsessional action was saying: 'No, it's not true. He had no need to feel ashamed in front of the housemaid; he was not impotent.'[11] The ritual expressed a wish – to deny her husband's impotence.

This interpretation of the ritual becomes more plausible in the light of information about the patient's general life circumstances. She had lived apart from her husband for many years but could not contemplate divorce. In order to avoid temptations to be unfaithful to her husband, she withdrew from the world and in her imagination she created an elevated image of him. The obsessional ritual had the meaning of repudiating her own potential criticisms of him. Freud comments:

Indeed, the deepest secret of her illness was that by means of it she protected her husband from malicious gossip, justified her separation from him and enabled him to lead a comfortable separate life. Thus the analysis of a harmless obsessional action led directly to the inmost core of an illness, but at the same time betrayed to us no small part of the secret of obsessional neurosis in general.[12]

Freud also notes that the interpretation of her symptom was discovered essentially by the patient herself, through her making the connection with a troubling event – one that linked to her most intimate areas of unhappiness, personal circumstances too painful to be tolerated in consciousness. Unconsciously she still struggled with the issues regarding her sexual life and her relationship with her husband, trying again and again to deny the humiliating reality. By generating a neurotic illness, her unconscious mind created a kind of solution to her conflicts, allowing her to live separately while preserving her husband's reputation, and moreover enabling her, in unconscious fantasy, to undo the unacceptable facts of her sexual unhappiness. This is typical of the way in which the unconscious mind can be quite ingenious in finding creative adaptations to mental conflict.

While the meaning of this ritual was readily understood by the patient, it is easy to imagine how the interpretation of the unconscious solution to a conflict may be strongly resisted in some cases. Undoing the unconscious disguise completely undermines the unconscious solution, thus exposing the individual again to whatever was the unbearable aspect of reality. For this reason, psychoanalysis has always been hated and feared (but unconsciously).

Freud and later psychoanalysts have described many ways in which human beings attempt to hide emotional truth from themselves. These are the *mechanisms of defence*,[13] which include repression (banishing from consciousness), projection (attributing to another person an unwanted aspect of oneself), rationalisation (concocting spurious explanations of one's motivations), splitting (keeping contradictory attitudes or feelings in separate compartments of awareness), manic defences (ways of denying feelings of depression) and many other subtle variations on these themes.

Such forms of 'lying' to oneself are both important and commonplace. They reveal how flimsy our conscious knowledge of ourselves is. However, there is a deeper reason for our dread of psychoanalysis – beyond its revelation of motivations that are unconscious. It is the threatening encounter with the utter 'otherness' of the unconscious – the life that dwells inside us, unknown to us, directing us and yet not speaking our language – the terrifying oracle that utters or mutters incomprehensibly during our sleep.

Dreams

The interpretation of dreams is the royal road to a knowledge of the unconscious activities of the mind.[14]

Dream analysis is the central problem of the analytical treatment, because it is the most important technical means of opening up an avenue to the unconscious . . . Dreams are objective facts. They do not answer our expectations and we have not invented them . . .[15]

The third point of access to the unconscious is through exploring the meaning of dreams. Freud felt that his major book *The Interpretation of Dreams*[16] was his most important work – and indeed the insights he presents there are profound and of lasting importance. Although psychoanalysis has branched in many directions since Freud's original theories and technical methods, all analysts make use of aspects of the understanding of the unconscious that is outlined in his book on dreams. Here, Freud offered not just a theory of dreams and a method of interpreting them, but also he discerned and dissected the modes of thinking and representation employed by the unconscious mind – modes that are quite different from those employed by our conscious mind.

Freud arrived at the hypothesis that dreams represented a disguised fulfilment of a wish – just as the neurotic symptom may do. This can be clearest in the dreams of children. Freud gives the following rather simple example of a wish expressed in a dream, which may be compared with the case described above, of the obsessional patient's expression of a wish through her ritual.[17]

A woman often dreamt as a child that 'God wore a paper cocked-hat on his head'. Taken on its own, without further information from the dreamer, there is no obvious meaning to this dream idea. However, the lady recalled that she used to have such a hat placed on her head at mealtimes because of her habit of looking furtively at her brothers' and sisters' plates to see if they were given more than her. The hat was meant to act as blinkers and as a means of shaming her in order to discourage this looking. It was not difficult for the dreamer herself to arrive at the meaning of the dream, through an idea that suddenly occurred to her: 'As I had heard that God was omniscient and saw everything, the dream can only mean that I knew everything, even though they tried to prevent me.'[18]

As in the case of the lady with the ritual of the table-cloth and the stain, the unconscious managed to repudiate an aversive aspect of reality.

In another example, a little boy, Hermann, aged just twenty-two months, was told to hand over a basket of cherries to someone as a birthday present. It was obvious that he was unwilling to do so. However, next morning he reported a dream as follows: *Hermann eaten all the chewwies!*[19]

Freud comments that these and other examples illustrate how children's dreams are frequently short, clear, coherent and easy to understand. Moreover, they often contain an obvious fulfilment of a wish (which usually includes the broader wish to be able to defy adult prohibitions). Freud draws a conclusion from this: that dream distortion is not part of the essential nature of dreams. However, there is a subtle form of distortion even in these simple childhood dreams, insofar as the latent thought or wish (for example, *I would like to eat the cherries*) is transformed during sleep into an experience (for example, *I eat the cherries*). Freud also noted that people who are suffering deprivation of physical needs, such as those who are starving (rather than merely desiring a cherry), may dream of those physical needs being met. He quotes the dreams of members of an Antarctic expedition, which would often be concerned with eating and drinking in large quantities. His own daughter, who had been forced to forgo food for a day owing to an upset stomach, dreamt of a menu, to which her name was attached: *Anna Freud; Stwawbewwies, wild stwawbewwies, omblet, pudden!*.[20]

From such evidence Freud postulated that dreams are a means of preserving sleep through providing hallucinatory gratification of otherwise disturbing wishes.

In these examples, there is a continuity between a conscious wish and the dream transformation of that wish into a hallucinatory satisfaction. Freud gives an example of a dream whose wish-fulfilling meaning is a little more hidden, although readily apparent on reflection: a man reported that his young wife had dreamt that her period had started. Freud reasoned that if she had missed her period then she must have known she might be pregnant. Thus, by presenting her dream, the woman was both announcing her pregnancy and at the same time expressing a wish that it might be postponed.[21]

Where dreams become more obscure is in their dealing with wishes that are frightening or associated with emotional conflict – wishes that are therefore subject to mental censorship and rendered unconscious.

Freud showed that in order to discover the disguised meaning of a dream, it is necessary to explore the dreamer's associations – his or her spontaneous thoughts – in relation to the various elements of the dream (since there are no fixed universal meanings of dream symbols). One relatively simple example of this process is the following.[22]

A woman dreamt that she wanted to give a dinner party, but had no food in the house except for a little smoked salmon. She thought of going out to the shops, but remembered it was Sunday afternoon and they would all be shut. She tried to ring up some caterers, but the phone was out of order. So she had to abandon her wish to give a dinner party. The woman reported that the previous day her husband had remarked that he was putting on too much weight and had decided to adopt a regime of exercise and a strict diet. This would include accepting no more invitations to supper.

With more resistance, she then provided further associations: that the day before she had visited a woman friend who was admired by the patient's husband, thus evoking some jealousy. However, she was somewhat reassured by the fact that her friend was very thin and her husband usually was attracted to a fuller figure.

Freud asked what the two of them had talked about. The woman replied that the topic had been her friend's wish to put on weight. Her friend had enquired: 'When are you going to ask us to another meal? You always feed one so well.'

Freud concluded that the meaning of the dream was now clear and he interpreted to the patient as follows.

It is just as though when she made this suggestion you thought to yourself: 'A likely thing! I'm going to ask you to come and eat in my house so that you may get stout and attract my husband still more! I'd rather never give another supper-party.' What the dream was saying to you was that you were unable to give any supper-parties, and it was thus fulfilling your wish not to help your friend to grow plumper. The fact that what people eat at parties makes them stout had been brought home to you by your husband's decision not to accept any more invitations to supper in the interests of his plan to reduce his weight.[23]

Freud then enquired further about the smoked salmon element in the dream. The patient replied that smoked salmon was her friend's favourite dish. It is interesting to note that in terms of its *manifest content*, the dream portrayed the non-fulfilment of a wish, while its *latent* (unconscious) content did, in fact, fulfil the dreamer's wish.

In this example, the patient's thoughts and worries about her husband's attraction to her friend, and her resulting hostility and wish to reject the suggestion of a dinner party, were almost certainly not entirely conscious. This constellation of thoughts and emotions would probably have been associated with some anxiety and shame – and were therefore subject to censorship. Because they could not be experienced directly, they found expression in the form of a dream.

Freud likened the dream censorship to the political censorship that was prevalent during certain periods. He gives an example of a 'highly esteemed and cultivated' lady's dream in which the dreamer appears to be about to offer sexual favours to the local soldiers, ostensibly as part of her patriotic duty.[24] The lady herself dismissed the dream as 'disgusting stupid stuff'. One feature of the dream was that at several points where the narrative would lead to an expectation of some explicit sexual reference there appears instead of clear speech a mumble. For example, a soldier said to her: 'Suppose madam, it actually came to . . . (mumble).' The dreamer then thinks: 'Good gracious, I'm an old woman . . . it must never happen that an elderly woman . . . (mumble) . . . a mere boy.'[25]

Freud points out that the dream thus shows gaps, not in the dreamer's memory but in the content of the dream itself. At crucial points – where this respectable elderly lady might give expression to her sexual desires and fantasies – the content is 'extinguished' and replaced by a mumble. Freud comments:

Where shall we find a parallel to such an event? You need not look far these days. Take up any political newspaper and you will find that here and there the text is absent and in its place nothing except the white paper is to be seen . . . In these empty places there was something that displeased the higher censorship authorities and for that reason it was removed – a pity, you feel, since no doubt it was the most interesting thing in the paper – the 'best bit'.

On other occasions the censorship has not gone to work on a passage after it has already been completed. The author has seen in advance which passages might expect to give rise to objections from the censorship and has on that account toned them down in advance, modified them slightly, or has contented himself with approximations and allusions to what would genuinely have come from his pen. In that case there are no blank places in the paper, but circumlocutions and obscurities of expression appearing at certain points will enable you to guess where regard has been paid to the censorship in advance.[26]

Freud hypothesised that if the wishes that arise during sleep are ones that might cause anxiety, guilt or shame, then the wish-fulfilment is disguised. As a result the meaning of the dream is no longer immediately apparent, in the way that it can be in the case of some rather transparent dreams of children. However, the dream may not be entirely successful in its effort to avoid anxiety. The dream may then contain highly alarming images and narrative.

Freud gives the following example of an anxiety dream.[27]

A young man reported that between the ages eleven to thirteen he had repeatedly dreamt that he was pursued by a man with a hatchet, and that he felt paralysed and unable to run away. In exploring his associations, the man recalled a story told by his uncle of how he had been attacked in the street by a threatening-looking man. Regarding the hatchet, he recalled that he had once injured his hand while chopping wood. Then he thought of how he used to ill-treat his younger brother, knocking him down and on one occasion kicking him in the head with his boot and drawing blood. His mother had said: 'I'm afraid he'll be the death of him one day.'

Finally, he thought of a memory from age nine when his parents had come home late and had gone to bed, while he pretended to be asleep. He had then heard panting and other noises, which had appeared to him 'uncanny', coming from their bed. Freud's explanation of this was as follows.

Further thoughts showed that he had drawn an analogy between his parents and his own relation to his younger brother. He had subsumed what happened between his parents under the concept of violence and struggling; and he had found evidence in favour of this view in the fact that he had often noticed blood in his mother's bed.

It is, I may say, a matter of daily experience that sexual intercourse between adults strikes any children who may observe it as something uncanny and that it arouses anxiety in them. I have explained this anxiety by arguing that what we are dealing with is a sexual excitation with which their understanding is unable to cope and which they also, no doubt, repudiate because their parents are involved in it . . .[28]

What Freud does not quite spell out here is that the young man's own sexual arousal from the bodily and mental changes of puberty would have stirred his earlier impressions and fantasies regarding sex and aggression. The overhearing of his parent's intercourse would have been frighteningly overstimulating for him, especially if it were imagined as a violent exchange that was both pleasurably exciting and terrifying.

Moreover, the young man's earlier childhood Oedipal wishes – to be his mother's partner and do away with his rival father (readily observable among young children within families) – would have been evoked, giving rise to fears of violent retaliation. The man with the hatchet (a common theme in horror films dealing with adolescent sexuality)[29] would thus have represented the fantasised vengeful father, as well as the bullied brother – the dreamer's own violent and aggressive impulses were coming back at him. The sense of paralysis would have expressed the experience of being unable to escape the mounting tension of excitement. In this respect the dream would have been a 'failure' in its function of avoiding anxiety.

Freud's formula that dreams are disguised fulfilments of repressed (repudiated) wishes that have been rendered unconscious is a brilliantly succinct explanatory hypothesis, and he gave a great many examples in support of this. However, the above example of the young man's hatchet dream points to the way in which this formula can become a little strained. Dreams seem to combine many different mental elements – fantasies, perceptions, fears, thoughts, creative ideas, as well as wishes. Perhaps another, rather looser, way of expressing Freud's insight would be to say that dreams attempt to deal with areas of emotional life that are troubling and involve conflict – and which are partly unconscious during our waking hours.

Bion[30] presents the rather intriguing idea that dreams themselves function as a 'contact barrier' between the conscious and unconscious mind – a boundary that both expresses and conceals the unconscious. Its function is to prevent the conscious mind being overwhelmed with 'stuff' from the unconscious. For this reason, the idea of interpreting dreams – of violating their cover – can evoke the dread of being driven mad. According to Bion's theory, something akin to dreaming (which he terms 'alpha function') – the transformation of sense data into *emotionally meaningful* visual, auditory, olfactory and tactile representations that can be 'digested' and contribute to the growth of mind – must go on all the time. The failure to dream is a serious matter. Bion puts it (enigmatically) as follows:

It used to be said that a man had a nightmare because he had indigestion and that is why he woke up in a panic. My version is: The sleeping patient is panicked; because he cannot have a nightmare he cannot wake up or go to sleep; he has had mental indigestion ever since.[31]

Is the psychoanalytic assumption that dreams are meaningful creations of unconscious thought valid in the light of current knowledge? With the discovery in the 1950s of rapid eye movement (REM) sleep and its correlation with dreaming, it was assumed by many psychologists that dreams were thereby shown to be merely meaningless images generated 'by noisy signals sent up from the brain stem'.[32] Those who took this view concluded that Freud's theory was so much nonsense. However, more recent research has revealed that dreaming is not exclusively linked with REM sleep; dreaming is not *caused* by REM sleep.[33] Indeed, Solms[34] has argued that the picture which current neuroscience shows of the dreaming brain is broadly compatible with the theory of dreams put forward by Freud a hundred years ago. Schore presents the view that Freud's general neuro-psychological theory of the mind was far ahead of its time and that it is only recently that neuroscience has caught up with his nineteenth-century insights.[35]

How dreams represent ideas: condensation and displacement

In addition to the distortion in dreams that is due to censorship and the need for disguise, Freud also drew attention to another source of their seeming obscurity. The language of the unconscious operates in quite a different way from that of the conscious mind.

Thoughts expressed through the conscious mind are organised in a sequential, more or less logical and grammatical form, roughly following certain linguistic rules.

This 'lawful' use of symbols is what enables one person to understand another when using the shared language. By contrast, the unconscious mind, especially as expressed in dreams, employs largely visual images that may combine many different meanings at once – these multiple meanings being *alluded* to, or indicated by fragments, rather than being stated explicitly and in full. It is as if a great many thoughts were broken into pieces or scrambled, then squashed together into a seemingly small bit of meaning.

However, this analogy does not do justice to the astonishing creativity and ingenuity that the unconscious mind shows in constructing appropriate dream images to represent a constellation of thoughts, desires and fears.

Freud used the term *condensation* to refer to this capacity to combine many different elements of meaning. He described the processes involved as follows:

Condensation is brought about (1) by the total omission

of certain latent elements, (2) by only a fragment of some complexes in the latent dream passing over into the manifest one and (3) by latent elements which have something in common being combined and fused into a single unity in the manifest dream.[36]

He comments that the simplest form of this condensation is where there is a figure in a dream who is a composite of various people.

A composite figure of this kind may look like A perhaps, but may be dressed like B, may do something we remember C doing, and at the same time we may know he is D. This composite structure is of course emphasising something that the four people have in common. It is possible, naturally, to make a composite structure out of things or places in the same way as out of people, provided that the various things and places have in common something which is emphasised by the latent dream. The process is like constructing a new and transitory concept which has this common element as its nucleus. The outcome of this superimposing of the separate elements that have been condensed together is as a rule a blurred and vague image, like what happens if you take several photographs on the same plate.[37]

A second feature of unconscious representation is that of displacement. Freud describes how this takes place in two forms: by the replacement of one element by a more remote element that alludes to the first; and by the shift of emphasis from an important element to one that is unimportant.

Later, the French psychoanalyst Jacques Lacan was to describe this process in terms of the 'sliding of signifiers'.[38] Whereas in conscious (particularly scientific) thought a word will have a fairly precise meaning, in the unconscious, meanings can slither easily from one representation (signifier) to another.

Yet another work of unconscious representation, particularly in dreams, is the transformation of thoughts into visual images and the substitution of an abstract idea by something more concrete. Freud gives the example of an idea such as 'adultery' (a breach of marriage), which is hard to represent in a picture, being portrayed by an image of another kind of breach, such as 'a broken leg'.[39]

Jung, an early collaborator with Freud, gives the following example – the dream of a thirty-one year old unmarried man.[40]

I found myself in a little room, seated at a table beside Pope Pius X, whose features were far more handsome than they are in reality, which surprised me. I saw on one side of our room a great apartment with a table sumptuously laid, and a crowd of ladies in evening-dress. Suddenly I felt a need to urinate, and I went out. On my return the need was repeated; I went out again, and this happened several times. Finally I woke up, wanting to urinate.

The dreamer explained the dream in terms of a need to empty the bladder during sleep. However, further meanings emerged as his associations were explored. Jung asked him to say what came to mind in connection with each element of the dream, as follows.

Seated beside the Pope: 'Just in the same way I was seated at the side of a Sheikh of a Moslem sect, whose guest I was in Arabia. The Sheikh is a sort of Pope.' Jung privately conjectures that part of the dream thought derives from the point that the Pope is celibate, while the Sheikh is a Moslem – the young man is celibate but would like to have many wives like the Sheikh.

The room and the apartment with the table laid: 'They are apartments in my cousin's house, where I was present at a large dinner party he gave a fortnight ago.'

The ladies in evening-dress: 'At this dinner there were also ladies, my cousin's daughters, girls of marriage-able age.' The man paused, displaying a resistance to continuing. Jung enquired about the young women. 'Oh nothing; recently one of them was at F. She stayed with us for some time. When she went away I went to the station with her, along with my sister.' He paused again and Jung asked what he was thinking. 'Oh I was just thinking that I had said something to my sister that made us laugh, but I have completely forgotten what it was.' Then he remembered. 'On the way to the station we met a gentleman who greeted us and whom I seemed to recognise. Later I asked my sister, "Was that the gentleman who is interested in – (the cousin's daughter)?"' Apparently the dreamer was also interested in the young lady but she was now engaged to the man alluded to here.

The dinner at the cousin's house: 'I shall shortly have to go to the wedding of two friends of mine.'

The Pope's features: 'The nose was exceedingly well-formed and slightly pointed.' Jung asked who has a nose like that. 'A young woman I am taking a great interest in just now.' Jung asked if there was anything else about the Pope's features in the dream. 'Yes, his mouth. It was very shapely. Another young woman, who also attracts me, has a mouth like that.'

Jung explains how the figure of the 'Pope' illustrates a common form of highly economic unconscious representation:

The 'Pope' is a good example of what Freud would call a condensation. In the first place he symbolises the dreamer (celibate life), secondly he is a transformation of the polygamous Sheikh. Then he is the person seated beside the dreamer during a dinner, that is to say, one or rather two ladies – in fact the two ladies who interest the dreamer.[41]

Jung enquired what came to mind in association with the idea of needing to urinate while attending a formal ceremony. The man replied:

That did happen to me once. It was very unpleasant. I had been invited to the marriage of a relative, when I was about eleven. In the church I was sitting next to a girl of my own age. The ceremony went on rather a long time, and I began to want to urinate. But I restrained myself until it was too late. I wetted my trousers.[42]

Thus, from the dreamer's associations, it can be seen that the dream deals with themes of his sexual desires, his conflicts about celibacy, his interest in two women, defeat by a rival in love, his wishes to be able to let go of his bodily desires and impulses (represented by urination), and his fears of humiliation and shameful loss of control (the memory of wetting himself in the presence of a girl). No doubt the dream would allude to many other meanings as well, and Jung notes that the analysis of the material did continue much further.

Jung's account is also of interest because he indicates the dreamer's hesitations (resistances due to censorship) which are apparent as his associations are explored. The wish to understand one's own dream is never without ambivalence – and a certain dread of encountering unknown aspects of oneself.

The cognitive unconscious: the mad logician and the mushroom of meaning

It will be apparent from the above discussion of dreams that the qualities of the unconscious mind are more than merely that of being not conscious. The conscious and unconscious minds operate according to utterly different principles – as different as the modes of reasoning and representation of a scientist/ philosopher on the one hand and a visionary artist on the other.

From the perspective of the reasoned and sequential mode of thought of the conscious mind, the cognitive methods of the unconscious mind seem like an insane mockery of our fragile strivings after logic.

Freud[43] identified a number of characteristics of the unconscious mind that are not found in the conscious mind.

1. Mutually incompatible impulses or ideas can exist without these appearing contradictory. Love and hate could both be expressed at the same time unconsciously, whereas the conscious mind would experience dissonance about this.

2. Meaning may be *displaced* easily from one image to another.

3. Many different meanings may be combined in one image – condensation.

4. The processes of the unconscious mind are timeless. Ideas are not ordered temporally and are not altered by the passage of time.

5. The unconscious pays no regard to external reality but represents internal psychical reality. Thus, dreams or hallucinations are perceived as real.

The implications of these points, if taken to their logical extreme, are rather startling. Whereas in conscious rational (especially scientific) discourse our language is ordered sequentially, one word following another, and each word having a more or less specific meaning, the process of condensation in the unconscious mind implies that all kinds of meanings may be presented concurrently without contradiction. The possibility arises, in principle, of a kind of total or ultimate condensation of all meaning and all potential. An analogy might be drawn with the contemporary scientific myth of the origin of the universe.

Prior to the Big Bang, all matter would be condensed into a point containing all potential forms and manifestations of matter and energy. We could picture the deepest unconscious mind as like this 'point', continually pouring out explosions of emotional meaning which then increasingly expand and differentiate as they manifest in consciousness. (We can never be in a position to know with any certainty how the universe began since we were not present at the time. The Big Bang theory could be essentially anthropomorphic mythology based on the structure of the human mind and the origin of our conscious thoughts.)

Freud seems to hint at something like this point of ultimate potential meaning in the following remarkable passage from *The Interpretation of Dreams.*

There is often a passage in even the most thoroughly interpreted dream which has to be left obscure; this is because we become aware during the work of interpretation that at that point there is a tangle of dream-thoughts which cannot be unravelled and which moreover adds nothing to our knowledge of the content of the dream. This is the dream's navel, the spot where it reaches down into the unknown. The dream-thoughts to which we are led by interpretation cannot, from the nature of things, have any definite endings; they are bound to reach out in every direction into the intricate network of our world of thought. It is at some point where this meshwork is particularly close that the dream-wish grows up, like a mushroom out of its mycelium.[44]

Freud uses startling analogies here: the dream's navel – 'the spot where it reaches down into the unknown' – and the comparison with a mushroom growing out of its mycelium. These do suggest an ultimately hidden and unknowable source, a point containing, or leading to, all meaning.

As Freud implies, a dream can never be fully interpreted because the dream's associations would ultimately lead to every other association in every conceivable direction of a network (the mycelium) of thoughts and meanings – as one signifier leads endlessly to another.

A modern association to the idea of 'mushroom' might be the mushroom cloud of an atomic bomb. Is a mushroom a kind of 'explosion' of growth? Could we conceive that a dream is a kind of 'explosion' from the unconscious – arising at points of particular density and tension in the meshwork of meaning?

It will be apparent that the distinction between the relatively fixed meanings employed by the conscious mind and the very fluid quality of the meanings apparent in unconscious thought is not an absolute one. Poetry obviously draws heavily on the same processes of imagery and condensation of meaning found in dreams. Similarly, visual art may present an image to convey a welter of meanings simultaneously. Even scientific thought may make use of metaphor – Freud's reference to the 'navel' of a dream being an excellent example.

Freud expressed his insights into unconscious processes largely in terms of his instinct theory – his portrayal of the shifting investments (cathexis) of ideas with instinctual energy. He postulated that in the conscious mind these cathexes are relatively fixed, but in the unconscious mind they are relatively mobile, easily moving from one idea to another.

This theory of instinctual cathexis will seem rather obscure to the contemporary reader and in fact is rarely (if ever) used by psychoanalysts today. However, what remains timelessly valuable in Freud's observations are the following two points.

1. The unconscious does operate with a different 'logic' to that of the conscious mind.

2. The cognitive processes of the unconscious mind are determined partly by the interplay of conflicting emotional forces (psychodynamics).

Others have since clarified further the nature of the cognitive processes employed by the unconscious mind, and how these are apparent not only in dreams but also in schizophrenic and other psychotic states.

One point that Freud did not articulate, but is

implicit in both Jung's idea of the 'collective unconscious' and Lacan's[45] concept that the unconscious is
structured as a language, is that the unconscious does
draw upon the pre-existing and externally existing
words, images and cultural references. Thus, the
unconscious is both personal and transpersonal.

The unconscious mode of thought in psychotic states

Silvano Arieti, who wrote arguably the finest book
ever on schizophrenia – *Interpretation of Schizophrenia* – examined psychotic and dream thought in
considerable detail.[46] He found that many of the
peculiarities of thought which Freud had found in
dreams and which were also displayed by schizophrenic patients could be accounted for by the
following principle.

*That the unconscious mind and the mind of the
schizophrenic person may perceive two or more things
as identical if they have some kind of associated
attributes which are identical.*

The reasoning might be along the lines of: Bill is a
British citizen; the prime minister is British; therefore
Bill is the prime minister – Bill and the prime minister

are regarded as identical because they have identical attributes of both being British.

Arieti gives the example of a patient who thought she was the Virgin Mary.[47] Her reasoning was:

The Virgin Mary was a virgin; I am a virgin; therefore I am the Virgin Mary.

It was also apparent that her arriving at this delusional idea was motivated by her wish to deny her feelings of inadequacy and assert her identity with her ideal of femininity. Thus, the delusion depended on both a degraded form of logic and psychodynamic motivations.

The early investigator of schizophrenia, Eugene Bleuler, gave the example of a patient who was preoccupied with his wish for freedom and believed he was Switzerland.[48] His reasoning was:

Switzerland loves freedom; I love freedom; therefore I am Switzerland.

The principle described by Arieti, of the unconscious and schizophrenic logic of identification of predicates, can be used to describe the formation of common dream symbols. For example, a snake, a cigar or a pen in a dream may symbolise a penis on the basis of a similarity of shape: a snake and a penis may be long and thin; therefore a snake is a penis. A box or a jewel case may represent a vagina because all are cavities.

Similarly, if a dream is representing an experience of the previous day, one attribute of the experience may be taken as the basis of a representation by an image that also possesses that attribute. An instance of this might be if a patient has experienced the psychotherapist as somewhat intrusive during a particular session and that night has a dream of being raped. The unconscious cognition here would be:

My therapist was violating me in his comments today. A rape is a violation. Therefore the therapist is a rapist [and indeed a 'therapist' is 'the rapist'!].

These symbolic functions are not, of course, limited to dreams and schizophrenic thought. The story of Bill Clinton and the cigar provided a joke that required no explanation. A TV advertisement in which a beautiful young woman sensuously licks a stick of chocolate makes use of allusions that are scarcely unconscious for most viewers. Picture language, cartoons, religious iconography and so on employ similar means.

The richness of language and culture depends on an

interplay between primary and secondary process cognition. However, for the schizophrenic patient the primary process mode of cognition may intrude into the capacity for secondary process logic, with the result that apparent metaphors are used but their abstract and 'as if' quality is lost. For example, a patient who was being kept under close observation in a psychiatric hospital stated her belief that she was in prison. Superficially this might have appeared a metaphor, a way of expressing her sense of her freedom being restricted. But on enquiry it became apparent that she believed she was actually and literally in a prison. There is here a failure of the capacity for abstract thought: the more abstract idea of a situation being *like* a prison becomes the more concrete idea of being *literally* a prison.

Disturbances of normal reasoning can also be revealed through the Rorschach inkblot test – where the subject is shown a series of coloured inkblots on cards, then asked what he or she perceives and to give reasons for those perceptions.

One patient kept seeing penises, vaginas and breasts in the inkblots and indignantly asked the psychologist: 'Doctor, why are you showing me all these dirty pictures?' For this patient the quality of looking *like* a sexual part of the body became instead equivalent to an *actual* picture of a sex organ. The degradation of logic was combined with the mental defence of projection, so that the sexual preoccupations were attributed to the psychologist rather than recognised as the patient's own.

Rapaport[49] gives the example of a patient who pointed to a coloured area of one of the inkblot cards and said: 'This bloody little splotch here – it's that bloody island where they had so many revolutions.'

Here the patient sees a patch of ink which looks like an island on a map; he sees also the red colour which he associates with blood, then fuses the two ideas to form the idea of a 'bloody island', and finally identifies it as a particular island where there were revolutions, which presumably were bloody. Rapaport referred to such instances of the loss of appropriate boundaries between concepts as 'contaminations'.

These various examples illustrate how psychotic patients may be trapped in a degraded form of cognition that does not work for them in negotiations with a world operating essentially according to conventional logic. For such patients words are no longer treated as symbols – that is, signifiers of objects that are absent – but instead are regarded as objects themselves. When a patient is in this state of cognition, the sound of the psychotherapist's voice may become more important than the *meanings* of the words; or the therapist' s name may be repeated over and over as a source of reassurance. Thinking has become *concrete*.

Segal,[50] in her discussion of what she calls 'symbolic equations', gives the example of a schizophrenic patient who was asked by his doctor why he had stopped playing the violin. He replied indignantly: 'Why? Do you expect me to masturbate in public?' While it would be quite normal for a *dream* of playing the violin to represent masturbation – the violin unconsciously symbolising a penis – it is quite a different matter if it has that meaning in waking life.

The loss of capacity for abstract metaphor in psychosis is like a situation in which the actors in a play or film suddenly run off the stage or out of the screen and begin killing or raping the audience; the 'frame' that states this is 'as if' is lost.[51]

Various psychoanalysts have drawn attention to the way in which the structure of thought itself (as opposed to its content) is altered in psychosis. What is a matter of some debate is the question of whether this reflects a fundamental deficit (with neuropsychological underpinnings) or an active defence against the awareness of unbearable mental conflict (or indeed a combination of these factors).[52]

A related problem is that schizophrenic patients may experience difficulties both in being properly asleep and being fully awake.[53] The dreaming mind is not properly confined to sleep. It can be as if the person is dreaming while awake. Unconscious modes of cognition have invaded the conscious mind, with dire consequences for the capacity to understand and communicate with others.

On the other hand, it must be emphasised that a too exclusive reliance on purely secondary process, logical and rational language, would appear both dull and abnormal. The emotional colour of our language, art and culture depends on the contained penetration of the unconscious mode of thought into our waking life. Some intuitively or artistically gifted individuals may possess an unusual access to the normally unconscious, or primary process, modes of cognition. If contained and harnessed, the primary process is the source of creativity, but if unleashed it can overpower and destroy the capacity for rational thought. Here lies the fine line between genius and madness.

Psychotic expulsion

To the extent that psychosis involves mechanisms of defence, a manoeuvre more radical than repression and related forms of disguise and self-deception must be involved. Normally, a content of the mind that has been rendered unconscious may reappear in a disguised symbolic form – in a dream, for example. It remains within a symbolic register, albeit disguised or encoded.

In psychosis, however, it is sometimes as if there has been an attempt to eject the objectionable content entirely from the mind, leaving a kind of hole in the fabric of representation. The ejected content may then return in the form of an experience of malevolent hallucination, continually rattling the psychic window. While dreams during sleep are a normal mode of representation, hallucinations while awake are not.

Freud noted, however, that psychosis is not restricted to those labelled mentally ill:

[E]*ach one of us behaves in some one respect like a paranoic, corrects some aspect of the world which is unbearable to him by the construction of a wish and introduces this delusion into reality.*[54]

Unconscious representations in everyday life

Just as dreams may represent an unconscious comment on a current situation in the dreamer's life, so we can

also discern other forms of unconscious communication and representation that take place continually.
These employ the same mechanisms of representation that are employed in dreams. Unconscious
meanings are disguised and displaced, and use
metaphor and imagery – or, as Robert Langs puts it,
they are 'encoded'.[55]

Very common instances of this are those situations
where a person is feeling angry and critical with
someone but suppresses these feelings because it
might be painful or anxiety-evoking to acknowledge
them.

Such conflicts over anger or criticism usually occur
in relation to someone who has an emotional significance to the person – such as a parent, a spouse, a boss
and so on. Under these circumstances, what usually
happens is that the suppressed feelings are communicated unconsciously in a disguised and displaced form
– for example, by expressing criticism of someone
else. Sometimes this disguised communication is done
consciously and intentionally; it is then called
'hinting'.

A student social worker's supervisor told her that
she was unexpectedly going to be away for a couple
of weeks. The student's overt response was one of
acceptance and an assurance that she could manage

without supervision for this period. However, she then went on to mention a case she had heard of from a colleague, in which a mother had left her young toddler child at home while she went out to the local shops. The toddler had woken up and had been severely injured falling down stairs.

The unconscious communication is clear: the supervisor is unconsciously experienced as a neglectful and abandoning mother, while the student is represented as a toddler who cannot take care of herself and who might suffer a catastrophe if left alone. The reference to falling down stairs expresses the student's sense of not being held securely and protected from danger.

Thus, *consciously* the student speaks as if she is an adult who can manage without supervision quite adequately for a couple of weeks; *unconsciously* she is accusing the supervisor of criminal neglect of her parental responsibilities.

Langs[56] gives an example of a man (Larry) who was called into the office of his boss (Ken) and told that unfortunately he was to be made redundant. After a factual discussion of the situation, Larry suddenly stared at his boss and remarked: 'You know, the way you look now makes me think of a picture of a man in today's newspaper. There is a really strong resemblance. He murdered his boyfriend; they were homosexuals. He will probably get the electric chair.'

On the surface, these comments do not seem to fit the context of the discussion about being fired and appear superficially confusing. Nevertheless, it is not difficult to see the unconsciously encoded message. Langs explains what is going on here.

> It appears that Larry is under a strong compulsion to express and defend against an unconscious perception of his boss as a killer, and of his own wish to murder his boss in turn. The allusion to homosexuality touches upon unconsciously perceived (and never at all conscious) indications of a latent homosexual and seductive set of feelings in Ken towards Larry, and in Larry towards Ken. It appears that Larry is unconsciously (via an encoded expression) suggesting that a critical source of the decision to fire him involves these unconscious homosexual conflicts. Clearly, these are all powerful raw messages, many of which Larry was entirely unaware of; they required automatic and unconscious encoding in order to be communicated in disguised (displaced) form.[57]

Unconscious representations may also take the form of enactments. For example, Langs[58] describes the case of a man whose wife had separated from him and had locked him out of the house. He inadvertently locked himself out of his car and had to make a forced entry. The actions – of locking himself out and forcing his way back in – were an unconscious enactment of the situation with his wife and his rageful wish to re-enter his home. Langs adds that at a deeper level this could also be seen as expressing his wish to assault and penetrate his wife.

A formula begins to emerge here as we consider encoded unconscious representation and communication. It is that emotional meanings are encoded unconsciously if they are experienced as too dangerous or frightening to be represented or communicated consciously. Encodings may take various forms – including imagery, dreams, daydreams, enactments, ambiguous and disordered verbal messages, slips of the tongue, and emotional or neurotic symptoms of various kinds.

Warnings and advice from the unconscious

Although Freud considered that dreams are merely attempts to preserve sleep by organising, containing and disguising potentially disturbing unconscious wishes, most psychoanalysts and therapists find that dreams can often appear also to be *communications* from the unconscious. This is actually a more Jungian than Freudian notion, but in this respect, psycho-analytic therapists in general, even when trained in the tradition deriving from Freud, have become more 'Jungian'.

Dreams may reveal astonishing intelligence and creative ingenuity, provoking thought about their meaning – and in this way can stir a person to reflect on aspects of his or her life that may be neglected in conscious preoccupations. Moreover, this communicative function of dreams seems to increase often when a person is having therapy or analysis.

Radha[59] gives the following example of a woman's dream.

I saw myself in a train station, preparing to take a trip on my own. But I had five suitcases and nobody to help me with them. When I woke up I had the strong feeling that I really wanted to leave, but I simply didn't know if could manage the heavy baggage. So I began to think that perhaps I would not go.

As this was explored in therapy, the woman realised that the dream was expressing her repressed desire to leave her marriage, combined with her fear that if she were to do so she would not be able to look after her five children, represented by the five suitcases. A dream of this kind expresses an unconscious thought (which includes a wish) and potentially draws it to the attention of the conscious mind.

Sometimes the warning function of a dream is startlingly apparent. A man, who was feeling drawn ever deeper into an affair with a highly attractive and seductive woman, dreamt that he was climbing a mountain, but left the path and his companion in order to admire and smell an extraordinarily beautiful rose. As he drank in the glorious scent he noticed that the ground in which the rose was growing was actually stinking manure. Moreover, he found his feet slipping as he stumbled near to a cliff edge where he could fall to his death. At this point he awoke. The meaning – and the message – is obvious.

Unconscious representations of frightening reality

It sometimes happens that a dream will represent a frightening situation that is known unconsciously but is being ignored or denied by the conscious mind. Jung gives an example of a seventeen year old girl who presented with symptoms that could either be of an organic illness or of hysteria. He asked if she remembered any dreams and the girl replied that she frequently had terrible nightmares. She then narrated the following two dreams.[60]

1. *I was coming home at night. Everything is as quiet as death. The door into the living room is half open, and I see my mother hanging from the chandelier, swinging to and fro in the cold wind that blows in through the open windows.*

2. *A terrible noise broke out in the house at night. I get up and discover that a frightened horse is tearing through the rooms. At last it finds the door into the hall, and jumps through the hall window from the fourth floor into the street below. I was terrified when I saw it lying there, all mangled.*

In Jung's commentary on this dream he elaborates on the unconscious metaphors of the images of 'mother' and 'horse'. Although framed in terms of his theory of archetypes and the 'collective unconscious' – innate forms of representation found universally in the human psyche – this appreciation of the way in which a dream may use metaphor would be congruent with the perspectives of most analysts (even if the meanings derived would vary). The usual clinical practice is to allow the images of the dream to resonate with the associations of both the patient and analyst, rather like listening to poetry. There is no one definitive meaning of a dream.

Jung's own thoughts were as follows. He notes that 'mother' and 'horse' in the dream both commit suicide. The image of a horse may represent the forceful animal aspect of the psyche, the unconscious, the instincts. Mother may represent origins, the body, the nourishing vessel.

Jung concludes that the two dreams are expressing the same idea: 'The unconscious life is destroying itself' and 'The animal life is destroying itself'.[61] He adds: 'Both dreams point to a grave organic disease with a fatal outcome. This prognosis was soon confirmed.'[62]

Various realms of the unconscious

Of course, Freud was not the first to discover the unconscious mind.[63] Novelists and playwrights have long alluded to our human tendency for self-deception and to be unaware of our true motivations. Those practising hypnosis in the nineteenth century knew that a person could be programmed to carry out a particular action and be unconscious of the source of the impulse.

More recently, cognitive psychologists have been happy to study non-conscious processing of information[64] and have even attempted experimental studies of unconscious psychodynamics.[65]

However, Freud was the first to study systematically the *dynamic* unconscious, which has remained predominantly the province of psychoanalysis. This concerns the process whereby unacceptable or frightening contents of the mind (wishes, thoughts, perceptions) are banished from conscious awareness, but continue to exert an influence, either by pushing to re-emerge into consciousness or by finding displaced and disguised expression through psychological symptoms, dreams, slips of the tongue or somatic disorders (physical illness). In addition to identifying the dynamic unconscious, Freud made a start on describing the peculiar modes of thought and representation of the unconscious mind.

However, there are other important realms of the unconscious. Stolorow and Atwood[66] have described two other forms in addition to the dynamic unconscious. One of these is the *prereflective unconscious*, which consists of the recurrent patterns, or *organising principles*, whereby a person perceives his or her relationships with others. For example, a patient in psychotherapy continually indicated her assumption that the therapist wished to turn her into a particular kind of person, while she in turn wished to rebel against this perceived pressure to mould her. She also seemed to experience people in other areas of her life as trying to control her. Moreover, at times she appeared to want to control the therapist by, for example, proposing all kinds of rules about what kinds of comments he was allowed to make.

Her recurrent organising principle, which determined her experience of herself in relation to others, was an assumption that the other person will try to control her – and that the only alternative is for her to control the other person. This organising principle appeared to be derived from experiences with her mother, whom she felt had established a life scenario for her even before she was born.

The notion of the prereflective unconscious is actually quite similar to Freud's concept of the *transference*. This idea can be quite complex and is used in somewhat varying ways by different groups of analysts, but basically it refers to the way in which a person will spontaneously, but without conscious awareness, repeat patterns of relationship that are based on relationships with parents in childhood.

Much of the work of psychoanalysis is to do with exploring this transference in relation to the analyst.

It is unconscious, in that a person cannot be aware of the pattern except through exploring and reflecting upon what emerges in a relationship, but it is not *necessarily* repressed (although it may indeed contain repressed feelings, perceptions or wishes).

Is the transference (or prereflective unconscious) a kind of memory? Well yes, in a sense, it is a form of *procedural* or *implicit* memory.[67] Rather than consisting of a memory of facts or events, it is an expectation of what will happen in relationships, based on recurrent patterns in the original relationships of childhood.

Although there has been much discussion in recent years regarding so-called 'recovered memory' (and 'false memory'), the remembering of previously forgotten events plays a relatively small part in psychoanalysis, which, in most cases,[68] is much more concerned with the recurrent patterns of unconscious relationships. The Sandlers refer to this template patterning of unconscious relationships as the *present unconscious*, derived from, but distinguishable from, the relatively inaccessible historical experiences of relationships in childhood, which they term the *past unconscious*.[69]

However, Stolorow and Atwood describe another way in which harmful events in childhood can be denied access to consciousness, not because they are repressed, but because they never receive validation from the important figures in the child's environment and therefore cannot be acknowledged and thought about. They call this the *unvalidated unconscious* (which may relate to the concept of the 'presymbolic unconscious' mentioned earlier). An example they give is of a nineteen year old girl who suffered a psychotic breakdown.[70]

For several years the girl's father had sexually abused her when she was younger. This had been a secret between father and daughter. He told her she must never mention it to others because most people had not evolved to the point where they could appreciate this special activity, which he claimed was enjoyed by royal families throughout history. Moreover, the sexual abuse contrasted utterly with the outward appearance of normalcy, the family playing a respected role in the community and being regular church attenders. Thus, there was a marked dissociation within the family and within the girl's experience.

The sexual abuse remained concealed until her mid-teens, when another child reported the father's behaviour. Prior to a psychotic episode she had dreamt that she was standing in the countryside, looking at a structure like an outhouse. She looked inside and saw a toilet. The water began gurgling up through the toilet bowl, foaming and overflowing. The flow became more and more agitated until it exploded with unidentified glowing material, increasing without limit. She awoke in terror.

Stolorow and Atwood argue that the dream represents the breakdown of repression, such that overwhelming emotions which had been in the *dynamic unconscious* – represented by the underground material – are now bubbling up in a terrifying and uncontrolled manner. The dream represents an aspect of the *prereflective unconscious* in its depiction of a division between the world above (alluding to the daylight and public world of a respectable family) and the world below (the experience of incest and betrayal), connected by the toilet. A dream image of a toilet does, of course, commonly represent the disposal of unwanted areas of experience. The unidentifiable and undifferentiated quality of the glowing material erupting from the toilet represents the *unvalidated unconscious*, overwhelming experiences that could not be named, thought about and spoken about.[71]

It will be apparent from this example that the three forms of the unconscious described by Stolorow and

Atwood are, in practice, somewhat overlapping. However, the conceptual distinction between the dynamic, prereflective and unvalidated unconsciousness is helpful in drawing attention to different aspects of these phenomena.

Another important feature highlighted by Stolorow and Atwood's example is that repression is often best understood as taking place in a relational context. Areas of experience are repressed because they threaten needed emotional ties (especially that of a child to a caregiver).

Jennifer Freyd has a similar concept in her 'Betrayal Trauma' theory of forgetting of interpersonal trauma.[72] Repression can also be seen as an interpersonal process insofar as one partner in a relationship fails to offer validation of the other's experience in that relationship.

The neuropsychological unconscious

An exciting recent development is the convergence of psychoanalysis and the neurosciences (as Freud had always hoped), forming the new discipline of neuropsychoanalysis. This is providing many interesting perspectives on unconscious emotional processing. Oversimplification is inevitable in describing these, but basically what emerges is that the right side of the brain, with its specialisation in visual perception, imagery and emotion, is the basis of the unconscious mind.[73] The left hemisphere, specialising more in linguistic and sequential logical processing, is the basis of the conscious mind. It matures slightly later than the right hemisphere.

During the first couple of years, the right brain is dominant and is strongly attuned to reading the mother's face. Through the orbitofrontal cortex the right brain links the perception of the external interpersonal environment with the deeper parts of the brain responsible for the autonomic nervous system and for generating emotion.

Later, the linguistic left brain becomes dominant. This imposition of slower sequential linguistic processing eclipses the rapid and holistic emotional information processing of the right brain, and creates a consciousness dominated by thinking with language. One way in which repression could occur would be through blocking communication from the right to the left hemisphere, with the result that emotional information is not processed into verbal language.

The unconscious mind, mediating between the conscious psyche and the soma, retains the visual and holistic imagistic thought processes of the right brain. Psychoanalytic therapy probably involves a shift towards more right brain functioning in both patient and analyst during the session. Attention is drawn towards imagery and metaphor and other aspects of the language of the unconscious (the 'primary process'). The analyst listens with his or her right brain. This is in line with Freud's recommendation that 'he must turn his own unconscious like a receptive organ towards the transmitting unconscious of the patient'.[74]

Some analysts find that they often become sleepy or enter a dream-like state of mind for parts of a session, this alternating with other moments when understandings from the right brain are processed through the linguistic mode of the left brain (the 'secondary process').

The tendency towards either a left brain or a right brain mode of functioning may influence the bias towards one form of psychological therapy as opposed to another. Cognitive therapy is clearly a left brain activity (often preferred by men and by those of a 'rational' or scientific outlook), as opposed to psychoanalysis which rests fundamentally upon right brain receptivity.

A hierarchy of consciousness or multiple consciousnesses?

Freud's theory of repression implies a hierarchy of consciousness[75] and a metaphor of depth – as in commonly used phrases such as 'the deep unconscious', or 'buried in the unconscious'. Freud and Breuer[76] distinguished this *splitting of the mind* (repression) into consciousness and unconsciousness from *splitting of consciousness* (now termed dissociation), where there are alternating consciousnesses (as in Breuer's case of Anna O and the hysterical patients described by their French rival, Pierre Janet). However, a non-hierarchical model is required for those patients (often extensively traumatised) who show marked dissociation or splitting rather than repression.

Dissociation is a marked disruption of the normally integrative processes of the mind, such that what is known and felt in one state of mind is not experienced when in another state of mind. Some degree of dissociation is common among those who have suffered overwhelming trauma, whether in childhood or as an adult. It is also a core feature of what is called Borderline Personality Disorder. However, in a small number of cases, the dissociation may be so extreme that a person will experience his or her mind as divided into a number of alternating consciousnesses or personality states. These conditions are called multiple personalities, or Dissociative Identity Disorder.[77] Here the boundary of awareness is not between consciousness and unconsciousness, but is between the varying consciousnesses.

The recognition of dissociation is part of a trend among some psychoanalysts to place more attention on the shifts between states of mind rather than on the interplay between a conscious and unconscious mind.[78]

Interestingly, the French psychiatrist Pierre Janet, who was working at the same time as Freud at the turn of the century, had developed a sophisticated theory of dissociation based on trauma, which is highly compatible with contemporary understandings of trauma.[79] Freud's rival theory of repression became the more dominant notion, thereby eclipsing the understanding of trauma and dissociation for the best part of a century.

To understand the dynamics of the mind we need both the concept of repression (and related defences) and also that of dissociation in order to take account of the interplay between inner psychodynamic conflict and trauma resulting from external impingement.

The infinite unconscious

. . . the system Ucs. resembles a child who is learning to speak and who at times conforms to the laws of grammar and at other times ignores them.[80]

One of the most innovative psychoanalysts since Freud is Ignacio Matte-Blanco, who has brought his background in mathematics and philosophy to bear on the problem of understanding the unconscious. In his first book – *The Unconscious as Infinite Sets* – he argued that psychoanalysis has, in various of its developments, walked away from Freud's original astonishing insights into the ways of the unconscious mind.

Many of the later preoccupations of psychoanalytic theorists, such as mechanisms of defence, internal objects, attachment, ego functions, life and death instincts and so on, may be of interest and import-ance, but they can take attention away from an appreciation of the language and mode of being of the unconscious. This is evidenced, for example, in the way that some theorists, who are not themselves psychoanalysts, can take aspects of psychoanalytic ideas and build an essentially left-brain orientated theory of therapy which does not address the unconscious mind – for example, cognitive analytic therapy.

Matte-Blanco examined the mode of functioning of the unconscious, and presented a proposition that clarifies and unifies the diverse peculiarities of unconscious reasoning. This is that the unconscious follows a particular logic, although it is a very odd kind when viewed from the perspective of the Aristotelian logic of the conscious mind.

The unconscious adopts a principle of 'symmetry'. Whereas in our conscious thinking, asymmetrical relations are common – such as 'Paul is the father of Peter' or 'this leaf is part of the plant' or '2 o'clock is before 6 o'clock' – in our unconscious thought these relations may be regarded as symmetrical. As a result, Peter is also the father of Paul, the plant is part of the leaf, and 6 o'clock is before 2 o'clock.

Matte-Blanco[81] gives the example of a schizophrenic patient who sometimes complained that blood had been taken away from her arm and at other times that her arm had been taken away from her. Clearly, for her, blood *from* her arm and her arm itself were identical. This may seem like nonsense – and indeed it is from the point of view of the conscious mind – but all the characteristics described by Freud in his discussions of the unconscious and of dreams are explained by this principle – including, for example, the absence of contradiction and negation, timelessness, profound disorganisation in the structure of thinking, the part standing for the whole, condensation and displacement (where one thing is treated as if identical with another).

A further aspect of symmetrical thinking is that where there is categorisation of objects of phenomena within a particular 'set' (for example, mothers, breasts, forms of aggression or any kind of category imaginable), then the unconscious treats all the elements of the class as equivalent. This is because grouping elements into a category or set is in itself a form of symmetrical thinking (A is like B; B is like A), and the unconscious simply extends the symmetry into complete equivalence. As a result, the unconscious will perceive one mother, or father (and the analyst in the transference) as the same as all mothers, or fathers, and will also regard one form of aggression, or violation or seduction, as identical with the most extreme forms of murder or rape.

The 'logic' of this extreme or polarised thinking is as follows. Voicing a rude word is part of the category of aggressive acts; therefore all forms of aggressive acts are the same as a rude word (because the part is equivalent to the whole). Another way of putting this is to say that the unconscious deals in 'infinite sets'.

The attempt to consider the full implications of symmetrical logic can evoke something of the experience of confusion and difficulty with thinking that may be found in certain states of psychosis. However, as Matte-Blanco put it, 'The principle of symmetry is an external logical way of describing something which in itself is completely alien to logic.'[82]

The whole matter becomes a little more comprehensible when it is appreciated that thinking normally involves a varying mixture of symmetrical and asymmetrical reasoning. Purely rational and logical thought is predominantly asymmetrical, whereas the language of dreams contains much more symmetry.

However, common unconscious mechanisms of defence may rely crucially on asymmetry as well as symmetry. For example, displacement requires that one thing is treated as if it were another thing, but in addition the defence requires that there is some differentiation between these two objects in order that the disguise can operate.

Similarly, projection and stereotyping depends on symmetry (all Jews/Blacks/Whites/homosexuals are the same and embody all possible negative attributes) while simultaneously preserving asymmetry which differentiates self from other. Good thinking, whether for scientific or poetic purposes, depends on an appropriate mixture of symmetry and asymmetry. Too much symmetry results in thought disorder; too much asymmetry leads to a dry discourse that fails to resonate with our human depths.

The mixture of symmetry and asymmetry in thinking is about the degree of differentiation in perception. Asymmetrical thinking sees difference and individuality everywhere. Symmetry sees no differentiation. There appear to be *stratifications* of symmetry-asymmetry. At the deepest level of the unconscious, pure symmetry prevails. All is one and the whole is reflected in the smallest part – an insight as old as human culture. In the depths of the unconscious, in pure symmetry, we find the Godhead,[83] the awesome Other within – the 'Subject of subjects',[84] which can never be the object – the source of our being and fount of sanity and madness, of creation and destruction, of Grace and Terror.

Notes

Where no specific page references are given, it is because the references are to the works in general.

1. Freud, S. 1940. 'An outline of psycho-analysis', *Standard Edition of the Complete Psychological Works of Sigmund Freud*, XXIII, London: Hogarth Press, p. 286.

2. Langs, R. 1983. *Unconscious Communication in Everyday Life*, New York: Jason Aronson. p. 85.

3. For example, Freud, S. 1916. 'Introductory lectures on psycho-analysis', *Standard Edition of the Complete Psychological Works of Sigmund Freud*, XV, London: Hogarth Press, p. 34.

4. Ogden, T. 1989. *The Primitive Edge of Experience*. Northvale, New Jersey: Jason Aronson, p. 2.

5. For example, Skinner, B.F. 1974. *About behaviourism*, New York: Knopf; and Watson, J.B. 1925. *Behaviourism*, New York: Harper Bros.

6. Baars, B.J. 1988. *A Cognitive Theory of Consciousness*, Cambridge: Cambridge University Press; and Horowitz, M. (ed.) 1988. *Psychodynamics and Cognition*, Chicago: University of Chicago Press.

7. Freud, S. 1915. 'The unconscious', *Standard Edition of the Complete Psychological Works of Sigmund Freud*, XIV, London: Hogarth Press.

8. Freud, S. 1923. 'The ego and the id', *Standard Edition*

of the Complete Psychological Works of Sigmund Freud, XIX, London: Hogarth Press.

9. Mollon, P. 'In press', *Restoring the Fragile Self. The Healing Legacy of Heinz Kohut*, London: Whurr.

10. Freud, S. 1917. 'Introductory lectures on psycho-analysis', *Standard Edition of the Complete Psychological Works of Sigmund Freud*, XVI, London: Hogarth Press, pp. 261–4.

11. Ibid., p. 263.

12. Ibid., p. 263.

13. Brewin, C.R. 1997. 'Psychological defences and the distortion of meaning', in M. Power and C.R. Brewin (eds) *The Transformation of Meaning in Psychological Therapies*, Chichester: Wiley.

14. Freud, S. 1900. 'The interpretation of dreams', *Standard Edition of the Complete Psychological Works of Sigmund Freud*, XVI, London: Hogarth Press, p. 608.

15. Jung, C.G. 1984. *The Seminars. Volume One. Dream Analysis. Notes of the Seminar Given in 1928–30*, London: Routledge and Kegan Paul.

16. Op. cit.

17 Freud, S. 1916. 'Introductory lectures on psycho-analysis', *Standard Edition of the Complete Psychological Works of Sigmund Freud*, XV, London: Hogarth Press, p. 118.

18. Ibid., p. 118.

19. Ibid., p. 127.

20. Ibid., p. 132.

21. Freud, S. 1901. 'On dreams', *Standard Edition of the Complete Psychological Works of Sigmund Freud*, V, London: Hogarth Press, p. 646.

22. Freud, S. 1900. 'The interpretation of dreams', *Standard Edition of the Complete Psychological Works of Sigmund Freud*, IV, London: Hogarth Press, p. 147.

23. Ibid., p. 148.

24. Freud. S. 1916. 'Introductory lectures on psycho-analysis', *Standard Edition of the Complete Psychological Works of Sigmund Freud*, XV, London: Hogarth Press, p. 137.

25. Ibid., p. 137.

26. Ibid., p. 139.

27. Freud, S. 1900. Op. cit., pp. 584–6.

28. Ibid., pp. 584–5.

29. Ivan Ward. 1996. 'Adolescent phantasies and the horror film', *British Journal of Psychotherapy*, 13, (2), pp. 267–76.

30. Bion, W.R. 1962. *Learning From Experience*, London: Heinemann; reprinted in *Seven Servants*, New York: Aronson, 1977.

31. Ibid., p. 8.

32. Hobson, J. and McCarley, R. 1977. 'The brain as a dream-state generator', *American Journal of Psychiatry*, 134, p. 1374.

33. Mancia, M. 1999. 'Psychoanalysis and the neuro-sciences: a topical debate on dreams', *International Journal of Psychoanalysis*, 80 (6), pp. 1205–13.

34. Solms, M. 1995. 'New findings on the neurological organisation of dreaming: implications for psychoanalysis', *Psychoanalytic Quarterly*, 64, pp. 43–67; Solms, M. 1997. *The Neuropsychology of Dreams*, Mahwah, New Jersey: Erlbaum; and Solms, M. in press. 'Dreaming and REM sleep are controlled by different brain mechanisms', *Behavioural Brain Science*.

35. Schore, A.N. 1994. *Affect Regulation and the Origin of the Self. The Neurobiology of Emotional Development*, New York: Jason Aronson; in press. *Affect Regulation and the Repair of the Self*, New York: Guilford Press.

36. Freud, S. 1916. Op. cit., p. 171.

37. Ibid., pp. 171–2.

38. Leader, D. and Groves, J. 2000. *Introducing Lacan*, Cambridge: Icon Books.

39. Freud, S. 1916. Op. cit., p. 176.

40. Jung, C.G. 1974. *Dreams*, London: Routledge and Kegan Paul, p. 9.

41. Ibid., p. 11.

42. Ibid., p. 11.

43. Freud, S. 1915. 'The unconscious', *Standard Edition of the Complete Psychological Works of Sigmund Freud*, XIV, London: Hogarth Press.

44. Freud, S. 1900. Vol V, Op. cit., p. 525.

45. Lacan, J. 1966 (1977). *Ecrits*, London: Tavistock.

46. Arieti, S. 1974. *Interpretation of Schizophrenia*, London: Crosby, Lockwood, Staples.

47. Ibid., p. 230.

48. Quoted in Arieti, 1974. Op. cit., p. 231.

49. Rapaport, D. 1946. *Diagnostic Psychological Testing*, Chicago: Year Book Publishers, p. 338.

50. Segal, H. 1957. 'Notes on symbol formation', *International Journal of Psycho-Analysis*, 38, pp. 391–7.

51. See the discussion of art, illusion, frames and boundaries in Milner, M. 1955. 'The role of illusion in symbol formation', in M. Klein, P. Heimann and R.E. Money-Kyrle (eds.), *New Directions in Psycho-Analysis*, London: Tavistock. Also see Milner, M. 1950. *On Not Being Able to Paint*, London: Heinemann.

52. Grotstein, J. 1977. 'The psychoanalytic concept of schizophrenia. 1 The dilemma', *International Journal of Psycho-Analysis*, 58, pp. 403–25; Grotstein, J. 1977. 'The psychoanalytic concept of schizophrenia. 11 Reconciliation', *International Journal of Psycho-Analysis*, 58, pp. 427–52.

53. Bion, W.R. 1962. Ibid., p. 7.

54. Freud, S. 1930. 'Civilisation and its discontents', *Standard Edition of the Complete Psychological Works of Sigmund Freud*, XXI, London: Hogarth Press, p. 81.

55. Langs, R. 1983. Op. cit.

56. Ibid., p. 82.

57. Ibid., pp. 82–3.

58. Ibid., p. 86.

59. Radha, S.S. 1994. *Realities of the Dreaming Mind*, Canterbury: Timeless Books, p. 119.

60. Ibid., p. 106.

61. Ibid., pp. 107–8.

62. Ibid., p. 108. Dreams should not, of course, be taken as a source of reliable diagnostic information regarding a physical illness.

63. Ellenberger, H.F. 1970. *The Discovery of the Unconscious. The History and Evolution of Dynamic Psychiatry*, London: Allen Lane.

64. Dixon, N. 1981. *Preconscious Processing*, Chichester: Wiley.

65. Horowitz, M. (ed.) 1988. *Psychodynamics and Cognition*, Chicago: University of Chicago Press.

66. Stolorow, R.D. and Atwood, G.E. 1992. 'Contexts of Being', *The Intersubjective Foundations of Psychological Life*, Hillsdale, New Jersey: Analytic Press.

67. Mollon, P. 1998. *Remembering Trauma. A Psychotherapist's Guide to Memory and Illusion*, Chichester: Wiley.

68. An example of memory recovery and reconstruction of childhood trauma is given in Casement, p. 1985. *On Learning from the Patient*, London: Routledge, pp. 102–67.

69. Sandler, J. and Sandler, A.M. 1997. 'A psychoanalytic theory of repression and the unconscious', in J. Sandler and P. Fonagy (eds.), *Recovered Memories of Abuse. True or False?*, London: Karnac.

70. Stolorow, R.D. and Atwood, G.E. 1992. Op. cit., pp. 36–40.

71. Of course, a dream should not in itself be taken as providing reliable information about childhood events.

72. Freyd, J.J. 1996. *Betrayal Trauma. The Logic of Forgetting Childhood Abuse*, Cambridge, Massachusetts: Harvard University Press.

73. Schore, A. 1993. *Affect Regulation and the Origin of the Self*, New York: Jason Aronson.

Schore, A. 2000. 'Attachment, the developing brain, and psychotherapy.' Paper presented to the annual Bowlby Conference, London, 3–4 March.

74. Freud, S. 1912. 'Recommendations to physicians practising psycho-analysis', *Standard Edition of the Complete Psychological Works of Sigmund Freud*, XII, London: Hogarth Press, p.115.

75. Influenced by the theories of the neurologist Hughlings Jackson, a contemporary of Freud.

76. Breuer, J. and Freud, S. 1893–95. 'Studies on hysteria', *Standard Edition of the Complete Psychological Works of Sigmund Freud*, II, London: Hogarth Press.

77. Mollon, P. 1996. *Multiple Selves, Multiple Voices. Working with Trauma, Violation and Dissociation*, Chichester: Wiley.

78. Horowitz, M. 1988. 'Unconsciously determined defensive strategies', in M. Horowitz (ed.), *Psychodynamics and Cognition*, Chicago: University of Chicago Press.

79. Van der Hart, O. and Horst, R. 1989. 'The dissociation theory of Pierre Janet', *Journal of Traumatic Stress*, 2 (4), pp. 399–414.

80. Matte-Blanco, I. 1975. *The Unconscious as Infinite Sets*, London: Duckworth. p. 41.

81. Ibid., p. 137.

82. Ibid., p. 148.

83. Bion, W.R. 1970. *Attention and Interpretation*, London: Tavistock. Reprinted in *Seven Servants*, New York: Aronson, 1977 (see especially pp. 26 and 88).

84. Grotstein, J.S. 1997. 'Bion, the pariah of "O"', *British Journal of Psychotherapy*, 14 (1), pp. 77–87.

Select bibliography

Casement, P., *On Learning from the Patient,* London: Routledge, 1985.

Freud, S., *The Interpretation of Dreams. Standard Edition of the Complete Psychological Works of Sigmund Freud* IV & V, London: Hogarth Press, 1900. (Also published as a Penguin paperback.)

Langs, R., *Unconscious Communication in Everyday Life,* New York: Jason Aronson, 1983.

Langs, R., *Decoding Your Dreams,* New York: Henry Holt, 1988.

Malan, D., *Individual Psychotherapy and the Science of Psychodynamics,* London: Butterworths, 1979.

Matte-Blanco, I., *The Unconscious as Infinite Sets: An Essay in Bi-Logic,* London: Duckworth, 1975.

Matte-Blanco, I., *Thinking, Feeling, and Being,* London: Routledge, 1988.

Mollon, P., *Freud and False Memory Syndrome,* Cambridge: Icon Books, 1999.

Orbach, I., *The Hidden Mind. Psychology, Psychotherapy and Unconscious Processes,* Chichester: Wiley, 1995.

Segal, J., *Phantasy in Everyday Life,* Harmondsworth: Penguin, 1985.